TAMEKA'S NEW DRESS. First Printing.

Published by Creative Medicine: Healing Through Words,
PO Box 2749, Tappahannock, VA, 22560

Library of Congress Control Number: 2016939838

ISBN 978-0-9965324-6-4 (Hardback)

ISBN 978-0-9965324-4-0 (Paperback)

ISBN 978-0-9965324-5-7 (eBook)

PRINTED IN THE USA

Tameka's New Dress
Written by: Ronnie Sidney, II, MSW
Illustrated by: Traci Van Wagoner
Designed by: Kurt Keller
Edited by: Tiffany Carey Day, Bess Haile, and Francesca Lynn

Please visit www.nelsonbeatstheodds.com for information about books, apps, mixtapes, teacher's guides and more! Follow us on social media and use the hashtag #TamekasNewDress, #NelsonBeatsTheOdds, #NBTO and #iBeatTheOdds

www.creative-medicine.com

FOREWORD

It was spring 2005 and I was on the campus of Rappahannock Community College preparing to take Advanced Placement (AP) exams – the final step after a year of hard work in my AP courses to show I mastered the content and skills of the courses.

I remember wearing my favorite shirt; it showed the African continent in metallic gold. As I sat in my advisor's office awaiting my results on the exams I noticed a man walking by. He noticed my shirt and complimented me. After chatting for a few minutes, he introduced himself as Ronnie Sidney. While smiling ear to ear, he mentioned he was pleasantly surprised that I, from the small town of Tappahannock, VA, was embracing my heritage and unapologetically proud of the birthplace of humanity. It was hard for him to conceal his passion for Black pride and education.

Ron's infectious enthusiasm and passion is stronger today and is observant in the work he is doing in the African-American community. He works as a therapist with court-involved youth, travels and gives talks to differing audiences on how he overcame his learning disability, and recently published two children's graphic novels, Nelson Beats the Odds , which shares the emotional ups and downs of his own story, adding a healthy dose of perspective that he hopes will de-stigmatize the challenges faced by students with learning disabilities and Tameka's New Dress. Ron's biggest contribution is that he is sending the message to African-American children that it is OK, and even cool, to be intelligent and African-American at the SAME time!

His new graphic novel, Tameka's New Dress, resonated with me and I know it will for many others. Like Tameka, I have been persecuted for being a fair-complexioned, Black girl with "good hair". The assumptions held by people in the African-American community about fairer-complexioned Blacks (e.g., if you're light-skinned with "good hair", then you're arrogant) and those who excel academically are such that I have been condemned and accused countless times of "acting white". These stereotypes are but other means of dividing Black women.

Still today, despite the many successes of African-Americans, society equates being Black with being inferior. It's sad. As a Black, educated, articulate, professional and driven female, I cannot and will not subscribe to these stereotypes. I believe in and pledge my life to Black excellence.

No matter a person's complexion, we all embody the beauty of melanin and a legacy of Black excellence. In queens like Nefertiti, Nzinga, Nandi, and others, we should recognize and nurture their power and determination for establishing equality, every day. I encourage Black excellence by paving the way for more Black lawyers. Ronnie encourages Black excellence by delivering encouragement to African-American children through his writing. In his new book, Tameka's New Dress, Tameka encourages Black excellence using her poetry and new dress. Nelson encourages Black excellence by standing up for Tameka. Mesha encourages Black excellence by learning to love herself. And you can, too, because you are infinite, capable, and beautifully made!

Rebecca Knight
Juris Doctor Candidate
University of Cincinnati College of Law
March 2016

First Print 2016

TAMEKA IS AN 8TH GRADER AT KEMET MIDDLE SCHOOL. AFTER TAMEKA GETS INTO TROUBLE FOR PUSHING ANOTHER STUDENT, SHE'S SENT TO THE PRINCIPAL'S OFFICE.

QUOTE:

"I never told anybody; I just buried it as deeply as I could and kept people at an arm's distance. I never really let a person get too close to me...I was a kid, and I had no power or control over the situation. I really wish I'd had the strength and the knowledge to say something sooner" (Robertson, 2009).
- Queen Latifah, American Actress and Recording Artist, Abuse Survivor

FACT:

In 2014, child protective services (CPS) agencies received more than 3.6 million referrals involving more than 6.6 million children. The largest percentages of report sources of alleged child abuse and neglect were legal and law enforcement personnel (18.1%), education personnel (17.7%) and social services personnel (11%) (Administration for Children and Families, 2014).

TAMEKA BEGINS WRITING IN A NOTEBOOK....

Some nights I think about my daddy.
He died when I was three.
I know that he's in Heaven,
Smiling down on me.

I didn't grow up easy,
My life was very hard.
I use to go to bed hungry,
Then say my prayers to God.

Protect my brothers and me,
And keep us safe from my stepdad.
Please don't let him hurt us,
Whenever he's drunk or mad.

My prayers were finally answered,
When my stepdad went to jail.
But we had to leave our mommy,
Because she needed to get well.

I am a Queen,
Like Nefertiti, Nzinga and Nandi.
I will rise up like a Phoenix,
And leave my past behind me.

ONE WEEK LATER, TAMEKA'S GRANDMOTHER ENROLLS HER AT BLAND MIDDLE SCHOOL. TAMEKA MISSED HER OLD FRIENDS BUT LOOKED FORWARD TO MEETING NEW ONES. ON TAMEKA'S FIRST DAY OF SCHOOL SHE MEETS NELSON IN MRS. GRONKOWSKI'S CLASS.
WHAT'S UP? MY NAME IS NELSON.
HI NELSON, MY NAME IS TAMEKA.
NICE TO MEET YOU TAMEKA. IF YOU NEED ANYTHING...

NOTE:

"Colorism is defined as an intraracial system of inequality based on skin color, hair texture, and facial features that bestows privilege and value on physical attributes that are closer to white" (Wilder & Cain, 2011).

FACT:

The 2012 United States Census Bureau Current Population Survey reported that about 10 percent of all children in the United States lived with a grandparent. Of children living with their grandparent, aged 18 years and younger, an estimated 2.7 million grandparents were the primary caregivers for the children (Ellis & Simmons, 2014).

QUOTE:

"It actually probably saved my life. It is the reason why I am where I am today because my grandmother gave me the foundation for success that I was allowed to continue to build upon. My grandmother taught me to read, and that opened the door to all kinds of possibilities for me" (Academy of Achievement, 2010).
Oprah Winfrey, American Media Proprietor, Grandfamily

FACT:

Compared to other ethnic groups, African-American children are more often raised primarily by a grandparent. These children are also almost twice as likely to live below the poverty line compared to children whose grandparents are not primary caregivers (Livingston, 2013).

TAMEKA GRABS HER LUNCH AND SITS AT THE TABLE WITH NELSON AND JEREMY.

WHO DOES SHE THINK SHE IS? AN AFRICAN QUEEN?

NELSON AND LIGHT BRIGHT SITTING IN A TREE, K-I-S-S-I-N-G!

TAMEKA, JUST IGNORE THOSE HATERS. DON'T LET THEM GET YOU IN TROUBLE.

QUOTE:

"I got teased my entire school life. What they were picking on I don't even understand. It was my skin color [which was lighter than her classmates']. Then when I got older, it was about my breasts. But I'm not victimized—I'm grateful. I think those experiences were strategically put together by God for the preparation of being in the music industry" (Glamour, 2013).
Rihanna, Barbadian Singer and Song Writer, Colorism

TAMEKA BECOMES ANGRY AND STARTS TO BALL UP HER FIST. MESHA STANDS UP AND APPROACHES HER FROM BEHIND.

OH, YOU MAD? DO SOMETHING ABOUT IT!

NELSON AND JEREMY JUMP UP TO HOLD TAMEKA BACK.

SIT DOWN, I'M FINE.

YOU KNOW WHAT MESHA? I AM AN AFRICAN QUEEN. I'M BEAUTIFUL, INTELLIGENT AND PERFECT IN GOD'S EYES. THE WAY YOU FEEL ABOUT ME IS NOT ABOUT ME, BUT HOW YOU FEEL ABOUT YOURSELF.

The Golden Matriarch

Releasing the love her daughter believed unworthy to keep
A granny prepares herself for motherhood again
And a little girl cries behind a window weeping the tears of confusion and feeling her first pings of a misunderstood abandonment every Sunday
Her mother.

But life goes on...
With years of multi-colored culottes
And an overstock on white tights
Girl Scouts, Choir Rehearsal, Tuesday
And Bible Study every Wednesday Night
Leadership Academy every summer so I can be more like Christ
Jack & Jill, débutante balls, & fork & spoon placement so I can be more ladylike
Saturday morning chores
Clean the silver
Wash the dishes
Vacuum the den
Or get the switches.

School
As are without question
Bs are failing
Bring home a C and catch a whoopin'
Don't cry or scream
Lunch
Leftover fried chicken and moist bread
I used to trade for Fruit Roll-Up instead
or dumped in the garbage and went home never fed
Ashamed that she wasn't hip to Dunkaroos and Lunchables.

Or maybe she just thought that it wasn't good enough for me
Not as good as the piano lessons I received
Ballet or tap
African-American Female Institute at JMU
Gospel Music Workshop of America
And she even gave me knowledge I never knew
She exposed me to the disheartening facts of being black
Because of our history that she lived this wasn't fiction she was talking, this was fact
And today I am grateful for all of that.

Grateful for the cord she made me wear that kept glasses on my face despite my sheer embarrassment
Grateful for the foundation upon which she placed my childhood, for my church home has become my village
Grateful for the journals she gifted me when I failed to use my time wisely
Grateful that she taught me to walk with my shoulders back and my head held high
Even though at times, my chest, I would try and hide.

I am grateful for this golden matriarch that raised me from a childlike confusion into a more refined organized chaos.

I am grateful for a Granny's upbringing.
Tanisha Carter
Instagram: RoseInThorn Twitter: TanCarter

ACKNOWLEDGEMENTS

This project would not have been possible without the grace and mercy of the Most High.

To the loves of my life, Talisha, Mali, and Morgan, thank you all for your continued patience and love. Congratulations, Talisha, on earning your Associates Degree in Nursing from Rappahannock Community College.

To Imagine That! Design, thank you for bringing my stories to life and providing quality service. Special thanks to my editors and contributors, Tiffany Carey Day, Francesca Lyn, Bess Haile, Tanisha Carter and Rebecca Knight.

To my beautiful and supportive family: Ronnie Sidney, Sr., Gwendolyn Sidney, Cherlanda Sidney-Ross, Van Ross, Deandre Sidney, Sydney Ross, Endia Ross, Robert Patrick, Sarah Harris, Etta Wright, Gail Wright, Tony Harris and Gil Holmes.

To some very special individuals and organizations: Virginia Commonwealth University (VCU); Dean James Hinterlong, PhD (VCU); LaRon Scott, EdD (VCU); Adai Tefera, PhD (VCU); MP-NNCSB; Chuck Walsh; Emily Eanes; Richmond Association of Black Social Workers (RABSW); Kevin Holder; Daryl Fraser; Renata Hedrington-Jones; Virginia Department of Education; Anne Holton; Marianne Moore; Pat Abrams, PhD; Doug Cox; Martha Hicks, I'm Determined; Ruth Tobey, Essex County Public Schools; Kristen Bumgarner (KWPS); The Virginia Council for Exceptional Children (VCEC); Virginia Education Association (VEA); Martha Hutzel, Central Rappahannock Regional Library; Meldon Jenkins-Jones, Richmond Public Library; Karla Redditte (NBC 12); Claire Ingebretsen (Fox and Friends); Marianne Moore; Towanda Darden (EYPC); Ernestine Scott (RPS); Erica Coleman (RPS); Kimesha White (SMS); Essex Public Library; Richmond County Public Library; Portsmouth Public Library; Westmoreland Children & Youth Association; Kara Collins (CCPS); Gayle Sterrett (RCIS); Lakeesha Klu Atkinson; Joy Lawson Davis (VUU); Sean Miller; Shawn Long; Christopher Pitts; Karen Blanchette; Sean Powell; Derek Hence; Christopher O'Neal; Kelsee Scott; George Washington; Tammy Terel Carter; Margie Samuel; Rappahannock Community College; Reynolds Community College; Old Dominion University; Good Hope Baptist Church; MANUP.

To the rest of my family and friends, thank you for your donations, support, and words of encouragement throughout this difficult project.

In closing, I wish to dedicate this book to the memory of Afeni Shakur and Amy Joyner-Francis. #RestInPower #StopBullyingNow

CPSIA information can be obtained at www.ICGtesting.com
Printed in the USA
BVOW05*2010180816

459456BV00007BA/13/P